A Damsel's Diary

BEFORE THE COMMITMENT

VOLUME 1

MERCY FAKOYA

Published by Victorious You Press™

Printed in the United States of America

ISBN: 978-1-952756-24-5

For details email vyp.joantrandall@gmail.com
or visit us at www.victoriousyoupress.com

BEFORE THE COMMITMENT

Preface

A *Damsel's Diary* is a vision that God gave me in 2017. Growing up, I had a lot of questions. I have made a lot of mistakes, and I always wished I could have a "do-over." I still wish I could have a do-over now. Lol. Looking at where I am today, I can honestly say that things would be very different if I knew then what I know now. I would have made better choices. But thank God for my past experiences because they made me who I am today.

As a mentor, I have found that many young and older adults face similar challenges as I did. They struggle to answer questions such as, "What is my purpose in life? Why do I have the need to please others? Why do I have the desire to be validated by others?" The different phases of life cause them to make statements like, "I am old enough to make my own decisions," and "Nobody can tell me anything," and the list goes on. With these experiences (and ones that I haven't even begun to discuss), I always ended up at a dead end. The point of confusion. The point of "What do I do now?" The dormant phase! This phase was the most challenging phase for me. This was the phase where I had to decide to humble myself, recalculate my steps, make a change, or simply turn around and make amends where I messed up. With time, I understood how to navigate through the dormant stage, but I see that many are still stuck in this stagnant phase. An example is a forty-year-old woman who behaves as if she is still twenty-one, or a married woman who continues exhibiting immature behaviors. Many can also attest to meeting someone who had no vision and just lived life as it came.

After I received the vision of *A Damsel's Diary*, I asked God where He wanted me to start and inquired about His revelation for the book. In my eyes, I thought it would just be one book that others could learn from, but God told me this would be a series! It will have volumes! I asked God for more clarity concerning the book, and He answered me instantly. He used my sister, Debbie, to open my eyes to the blueprint of why He wanted this book written. He told me these volumes would break generational curses and bondages. God told me lives would be changed, and people will have testimonies because of the book's impact. He didn't stop there. God used my goddaughter, Sarah, to explain the format the book should take. He explained every avenue, street, and road in which the book should be constructed! By the time God finished explaining it all, I was overwhelmed, to say the least. They had no clue of what God was doing through them. They were just talking, but I heard God.

I am sharing this revelation with you because I believe God has something to say to you. He has instructed the Holy Spirit to take your hand as you journey along with *A Damsel's Diary.* God loves you so much that He doesn't want you to do it alone. He doesn't want you to mess up. He wants you to go through every stage of your life like a breeze! He wants to be there for you at your high and low moments. He wants you to trust Him as you hold his hands.

So often, we create a future for ourselves that was not according to God's plan. We make decisions without God's approval, and then we fail. God wants to walk this journey with you and show you the treasures that have been stored up for you. He wants to anoint you and watch you succeed. The only thing that you have to do is trust Him. Trust the One who has the answer to all the questions that linger within your heart. Believe in the One who has the blueprint to your life, the One who wrote every word in your book of life. His name is God.

So, as you take this trip into *A Damsel's Diary*, I pray your heart will be receptive to the Holy Spirit. I pray the vision for your life becomes clearer. I pray you are not afraid to trust God and trust what He has in store for you. I pray you truly surrender your life to Him, and I pray your life becomes a testimony for yourself and others.

This is *A Damsel's Diary.*

Prologue

To my darling, amazing, sophisticated, faithful, loving, and passionate daughters and nieces, you are queens, giants, and women who will impact the world - Miss Trinity and Miracle Fakoya, Precious, and Krystal Akinkunle. You will transform from the Damsel into the Proverbs 31 woman, full of passion and purpose. You will pursue, overtake, and recover all the blessings that your ancestors and generations may have lost, and you will conquer every land that you step on.

To every Damsel, every woman who is loved by God, to the young woman who has been degraded, intimidated, misused, abused, marginalized, and defamed, to the woman who is still trying to identify her purpose, and to the lost, found, and in between, this book is for you. As you flip through the pages, I trust that God will fill you with wisdom to conquer your journey in life and to pursue and accomplish your purpose.

Table Of Contents

Introduction 1
1. Purpose Over Passion 5
2. What's The Rush? 9
3. You are You! 15
4. Who Are You? 17
5. The Perfect Man 25
6. He Still Wants You 33
7. Addressing the Four P's 39
8. Distractions 47
9. When Will It Be My Turn? 55
10. Tune In To Your Now 61
11. Embrace Your Now 65
12. Calling 71
13. Trust In God 79
14. Defeat The Enemy Within 93
15. The Next level–Marriage? 103
Epilogue 109
References 111

Introduction

I know you are wondering why I wrote this book. I wrote this book because I believe you need it. When I look back at my past, I wish I would have had a guide to help me along my journey. Now, let me make this clear, what I have to say does not compare to what the Word of God says concerning your life. But I cannot deny the fact that it was easier for me to pick up a novel rather than the bible. Even at my current age, it takes pure discipline to pick up my bible every morning and spend time in the presence of the Lord. I believe my struggles in my singleness, and even now (in marriage), are also the same struggles that others face.

When I think about my life experiences, the errors I made, the hurdles I jumped over, I realize how desperately I needed a book like *A Damsel's Diary* to guide me. Yes, there were people available to direct me. Yes, other people's confessions were available to my ears, but there is nothing like sitting down, imagining, exploring, and digesting the words on the pages of a book. A book that addresses my secret thoughts and experiences and enters into the deep parts of my imagination, uprooting the thoughts of the enemy that has taken residence. Imagine a book that holds nothing back, no reservations. Many refuse to admit it, but I will. I needed help back then, and I still need help now. There is nothing like a stranger meeting you on the street, who begins to provide you with tools to overcome past hurts and shows you how to experience the present and future joy. To be honest, I don't want any woman to live in the uncertainty of what could have been. I want every woman to walk in power, passion, perspective, and potential. That's what *A Damsel's Diary* will do.

In this book, I share stories of women who have experienced various challenges in their lives. I discuss my response and provide tools and strategies on how to overcome those issues. I am confident that you will be able to relate to some, if not all, of the stories within this book, whether it happened to you or someone you know. To protect the identity of the individuals whose stories I am sharing, I have changed their names. My goal is for you to learn from these stories and make choices that will positively impact your life. It is my desire that as you read the words on the pages in this book, you will be ignited to live the best you! The words on the pages of this book are not just for intellectual entertainment. No, I have prayerfully written this book with you in mind. Yes, you! The Damsel.

There has not been one time that I picked up this book and did not invite the Holy Spirit to operate through my fingers. I understand the importance and the urgency of the message I am sharing with you, and I cannot afford to write this alone. I cannot afford for this book to be just a book that you read and then forget. So, I have submitted my hearing to the voice of the Lord. I have made myself available to be a witness to Jesus. More importantly, I have requested the presence of the Holy Spirit to pour forth through my heart, mind, soul, and fingers as I write for each and every soul that reads this book. So, don't be surprised if you begin to experience life-transforming moments. Don't assume that it is a coincidence when new ideas, thoughts, and imaginations come into your mind. Don't think for a second that the seemingly impossible strategy that God will download into your heart can never happen. Oh no, honey! Let me tell you right now, the Holy Spirit is all over the pages of this book, and He will lead and direct you as you read. He will begin to reveal the blueprint for your next step in this book. He will begin to break everything that has kept you bound. The book did not appear in your hands accidentally! Nope! God said, "Now is the time for you to spring forth. There will be no more delay! Enlarge your space! Make it bigger! Make room for the impossible. The Lord is on your side, and you will prevail." Selah!

Before I proceed, I want to pray for you:

"Sweet Jesus, I am thankful for my sister, who has chosen to read the pages of this book. I am thankful for her life and everything concerning her. I ask that You ignite a fire within her! A fire that will make her stand confidently with boldness and declare what You have given her in Your name. I ask that she realize who she is and how great she is in You. I pray she will experience Your love so much that she will draw nearer to You. I pray You expose to her, her true purpose and calling so that she will only walk in the shoes You have provided for her and not the shoes of another. I pray that You give her strength to lay down all the hurt and shame that has kept her bound and that she replaces them with joy and happiness. Through this book, I pray she will realize her power in You and walk in her purpose, for a purpose, and with a purpose all the days of her life. I pray that she makes herself available for Your transformation, in Jesus' name. Amen."

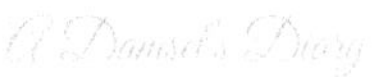

CHAPTER 1

Purpose Over Passion

There is a certain stigma that suggests women must be married, have kids, and achieve goals set by society by a certain age. While sitting on the opposite side of the table from a group of women, I listened to several of them speak about being single, having relationship issues, and how they either need to get married, are getting old, can't seem to find a man, have been waiting on the Lord with no luck, or are married and want to find a way out. I was not surprised by some of the questions people had asked them:

"How old are you now?"

"Are you dating anyone?" or "You're *not* dating *anyone*?"

"When is the wedding?"

"When will someone be a bridesmaid at *your* wedding?"

"When do you expect to get married and have kids?"

"Congrats on your wedding! When are you getting pregnant?"

"Are you only going to have one child?"

These are the reasons for this chapter. The notions about marriage and children have been so grounded in society that young girls grow up with these expectations. From childhood, they learn how to care for children when they play with their dolls. They learn how to cook and clean by watching their mothers and then practice in their toy kitchens.

Culture also plays a big part in this and is often a determining factor in the level of pressure that mounts as you become a woman. I grew up in an African home, a Nigerian family, to be precise. Now, funny enough, my mother never pressured me to have a boyfriend or get married. Actually, she avoided the subject altogether. I really don't know why, but I assumed it was because my sister had her first daughter when she was young. Another reason I assume she avoided the subject was because in her eyes, I was still five years old, and that would never change. Lol. Regardless of the reason, my mother never did the "pressuring" thing. There was no need for her to do it anyway because others had that shift covered. Many aunties, who were not really my aunties, would come up to me, call me, see me in the street or at church and ask me when I was going to get married. One of the most frequent lines that I heard was, "All your friends are getting married and having children. What are you waiting for?" Those words never phased me. I would just look at them, smile or frown, and say, "In God's time." It's so funny how my mother never had an issue with me not being married, but the people, mostly women, who I saw on an annual basis or so, had something to say! I'm sure you can add your story to the list too.

CHAPTER 2:

What's the Rush?

I have noticed that many women rush down the aisle for the wrong reason and end up living in misery until God's intervention. In contrast, others separate from or divorce their spouses. My heart aches for women who are so eager to rush into marriage without truly understanding the purpose, power, pressure, and pleasure of marriage. Some of them had been so eager that they fell into the trap of marriage and now feel stuck. Many are hurting inside but can't voice their feelings because they are afraid of what people will say. Many suffer in silence because they believe that it's just part of life. Everyone wants to please society! Everyone, subconsciously, wants to prove people right. How? You may ask. Well, because it is often said that you should be married by the age of twenty-five, so, you struggle to accomplish that. Your mother told you that you should be a doctor; you push yourself, without the passion, to accomplish that. Your best friend has a boyfriend, and you think that's what you need in your current season of life. So, you force yourself to dress in a certain way to attract a specific type of guy. We are always trying to please others, to prove them right.

Society has become an idol to many. You're probably thinking, *"That seems a little over the top, Mercy."* Does it now? The truth is, we were created to worship! That is our ultimate purpose. Who or what we choose to worship determines our idol. No matter what, we are worshipping. Every single day, we are worshipping. But my question is, what are we worshipping? According to the Oxford English Dictionary, an idol is "an image or REPRESENTATION of a god used as an object of worship, a person or THING that is greatly admired, loved, or revered." We unknowingly allow the thoughts of others to become a god in our lives when we seek their approval. Think about it. If you need to get a new outfit, you think about what the current trend is. So, you look at what celebrities are wearing and try to mimic them. Perhaps you want to post on Facebook or Instagram, you then consider who your target population is, and create a post that will engage them and cause them to hit the like button. If you want to become friends with someone, you might consider their popularity status before determining if they are "friendship worthy." If they're not popular, they're not your type. You want to attend a church, so you look for the biggest church with a trending pastor without considering the message they deliver.

In the above examples, God was not mentioned once, right? Exactly! Society has become a representation of God that many worships. We admire, love, and yearn for its approval. We only invite God into certain areas of our lives. He is allowed in our lives when we have struggles. We go running to Him when we need help. He's the "go-to person" after we've made a decision, and it starts to fall apart. We beckon for God's intervention after marrying a guy without His consent or approval. When all hope is lost, we plead for Him. That's good, but is that how you treat your best friend? I hope not.

God doesn't want to have a 'sometimes' or part-time relationship with us. He wants to be involved in all the decisions we make, even the tiniest ones. He wants you to involve Him in the outfit you want to wear, the guy you want to date, the plans you have for the day, the school you wish to attend, the job you're applying for, the words you say when someone upsets you. He wants you to tell Him how your day was, what made you happy or sad. This might sound crazy to you, but He's waiting for you to sit down and have coffee with Him. His ears are open to hear everything you have to say; and trust me, it won't be a one-sided conversation. He has things to tell you too! Things that you can't even imagine. He's ready to give you direction if you allow Him to carry you when you feel like giving up. He can be your confidant, your anchor, your best friend. For this to happen, you've got to allow Him to take His rightful seat in your life. Society cannot have its place in your life any longer.

There's nothing left to prove to society when you give God His rightful position. Stop comparing yourself to others. You are you! Think about it! You were born on a specific day at a specific time. Ask your mother. The pregnancy journey that she went through was one to remember. Even if you have siblings, there were some things during her pregnancy with you that made your journey different. Your birth was different. The pain she went through was different. You look different. Even if you are an identical twin, there are features, behaviors, and characteristics that make you different. There is no one like you. You are a peculiar, unique, and uncommon individual. So why must you follow the norm? Why do the standards that have been set by society matter? Who gave society the right to determine when you accomplish whatever goals you have in mind? Whose time clock are you going by?

Before you move ahead in this book, I want you to know that trying to attain goals because others have reached their goals is not the way to live a happy life. You and I can never live happy or successful lives if we are always merging into the next lane because our lane is not moving fast enough. Yeah, you know what I mean. You know that feeling you get when there's a lot of traffic. You get into another lane because that lane seems to be moving faster; however, the moment you get into that lane, it slows down, and the lane you left starts to move more quickly. The cycle seems never-ending. You move from lane to lane, and still, you're not getting anywhere fast enough. You get so irritated that you might just utter some unpleasant words to those who you feel aren't driving well. How frustrating! I have to be honest, though, the feeling you get in traffic may last for an hour or two, but when it's over, it's over.

You can't live life frustrated like that. There are no do-overs. We only get one chance at life. When it's over, it's over. So, make this promise to yourself. "I am no longer bound by the words of man. I will not allow the chatter to control my life. My time is my time, and God has already prepared my table for me in His time. I refuse to operate on someone else's clock. I trust you, Lord, that your plans for me are yes and amen. I am willing to let you have your rightful place in my life, Lord. Here's my heart, Lord. Please take your seat."

CHAPTER 3

You are You!

I'm here to tell you to STOP and BREATHE! You are different, unique, created for a purpose with your own timeline. Your purpose is too critical for you to work off someone else's watch. Your life is too crucial to be living by the checklist of society. You are you! You are not your mother, your sister, your girlfriends, your neighbor, or whoever else you are comparing yourself to. You are you! It is high time that you take your life back from the world and give it to the only person that knows how your life should be–your Creator.

I cringe at my past mistakes of trusting others before God. Instead of going to my Father in heaven, I would compare my life to someone else's and make conclusions based on my analysis. Now I look back and say to myself, "Mercy, what were you thinking?" Don't get me wrong. There is nothing wrong with seeking godly counsel, but it is imperative that you have a relationship with your Creator first so that He will order your steps and direct your path (Psalm

119:133). He will then reveal to you the next step that He has ordained (Joshua 1:3). Furthermore, He will show you who to go to for godly counsel (Proverbs 1:5).

Sis, you've got to live the life that God has given you. If you try to live your life based on someone else's timeline, you will fail because your name isn't on it. I believe that many people have lived and died without walking in their purpose. So, where am I going with this? You need to identify what your calling is and work towards it. You must make sure that everything you do will draw you closer to your calling, and this includes the man you decide to take as your husband. Marriage is not that simple, and it is a ground that should not be tread upon lightly. It is not for the faint at heart. It is not for the immature; neither is it for the unequipped. An African adage says, "If you run into marriage, you will run out!" It's funny that the same culture that stresses on getting married early is the same culture that has a proverb about patience. I need you to understand that the commitment you make in marriage will positively or negatively impact your purpose. So, I'm going to tell you again, STOP and BREATHE. The course that you will take in this life is completely different from your sisters. Don't be fooled by the noise. Ignore the distractions. Focus on yourself! Your God! Your journey! Your goals! Your dreams! Your desires! Your life! YOU!

CHAPTER 4

Who are You?

Your worth is so precious that He (God) transformed into the human flesh (through Jesus) to come and sacrifice himself for you. YOUR WORTH is beyond rubies.

Before you can continue *A Damsel's Diary*, it is important that you know and understand who you are. If there is anything that you do in this life, make sure this is on the top of your list.

We are so bombarded by the struggles and challenges of this world that our worth is clouded by LIES. We define our worth by what we see on TV, what our friends, family, and enemies say, by social media posts and likes, the trend, our environment, the music we listen to, the Netflix series we watch, our past, and present. The lies that have been downloaded into our brains since childhood are the devil's lies!!!! The voices are so loud and clear that doubting it seems unrealistic, especially when others verify the lies.

As painful as it is, these are the true lies that many live. Some go to the extent of questioning their existence, their purpose, and their worth. But I am here to tell you that you are WORTH IT! I am here to shatter the lies that have been buried in your subconscious. The Lord has sent me here to consume, by the power of the Holy Spirit, every demonic thought that has been feeding you with these lies. The Lord has brought me here to collapse every thought of doubt, failure, pain, anger, frustration, and the likes.

Many people are unsuccessful because they fail to understand who they are and who God has created them to be. Many people live in the shadows of others because they are afraid, ashamed, or unwilling to put in the effort to discover themselves. God does not want this for you. This is not His plan. Your purpose is not to be a sidekick or live life as part of the crew. Understand that with every word, there is a definition. The same also goes for every individual that exists on earth. Before God spoke the words, "Let there be light," in Genesis 1:3, He had a reason, a definition, and purpose for that light. He had already sketched out the assignment of the light. He strategically instructed the light to appear first because He wanted all that would come AFTER the light to behold His glory! The same goes for you. The Lord took His time and molded you into a perfect being so that all who encounter you will be able to see the glory He has placed on your life. He did this so you would be a blessing to the lives of all that are privileged to meet you and so you can walk this journey of life with purpose. So, who are you?

I want you to take a moment and think about the answer to this question. Who Are You? What makes you, you? After you have lost your job, you're no longer in school, there are no more friends around, and life itself stands still–Who Are You? If you are struggling with the answer to this question, it's okay. I believe that as you continue this journey, you will begin to pick up treasures from the Holy Spirit, which will define who you truly are. I would like to share some biblical truths about you before we continue.

2 Corinthians 5:17 (NLT)

"This means that anyone who belongs to Christ has become a new person. The old life is gone; a new life has begun!"

You have been birthed into the family of Christ. Once you accept Him into your life and take on His name, you are now married to Him. A new life is granted unto you. Everything old and of the past has been wiped away. Not only does your name change, but you receive a clean slate. Your name is renewed to impact your generation and leave a legacy.

1 Peter 2:9 (TPT)

"But you are God's chosen treasure[a]—priests who are kings, a spiritual "nation" set apart as God's devoted ones. He called you out of darkness to experience his marvelous light, and now he claims you as his very own. He did this so that you would broadcast his glorious wonders *throughout the world.*"

Now, this scripture is loaded and cannot be defined with a few words, so let me break it down for you.

God's chosen treasure

You are precious, valuable; you are priceless, the King's jewel, extraordinarily valuable, unique, like no other, God's excellence, His Masterpiece.

A Priest

Ordained, a minister, with particular authority, respectable, one with a special connection to God. A person of honor. A close worker of God.

A King

A ruler, one in authority, a god, a right inherited by spiritual birth in Christ, a monarch, the most important person at any event, a winner.

A Nation

A large aggregate of people united by common descent, history, culture, or language, inhabiting a particular country or territory. Although you are one person, He is telling you here that a nation intends to come out of you! God has designed it so.

Set apart

Peculiar, different, special, uncommon, preferred, approved, favored, reserved, endorsed, elected, separate.

Devoted one

Loyal, loving, faithful, trustworthy, steadfast, committed, dedicated.

Claimed

You belong, no longer an orphan, of value.

His very own

Belonging to a particular person and to no other.

There are so many other scriptures that have been written specifically to help you identify who you are, and I will introduce you to more soon.

Before you can invite someone to share your life with you, and this goes for anyone, you must make sure you are complete. Many enter relationships while they are still broken, incomplete, or desperate. Now don't get me wrong; there are people who get into relationships for the right reasons. However, for the majority, relationships happen because they believe a void needs to be filled. It is important to understand that relationships also break because the initial need was not fulfilled, or other potholes were created along the journey. The person could not fulfill the other person's needs. This is why it is vital to know who you are before introducing yourself to someone, get involved in a relationship, or anything of that nature. Think about it. What will you offer the other person? Uncertainty? Confusion? Pain? Insecurities? It would be an injustice to you and others.

There is so much that you have to offer, and there is so much that God has in store for you, but He needs you to identify who you are. The delivery guy cannot deliver packages unless his truck is filled. The gas station cannot dispense gas unless fuel has been poured into the filling station fuel tanks. You cannot deliver what God wants you to deliver until you allow Him to pour into you. He needs to prepare you for every stage that you will encounter. He needs you to understand who you are so you will not sell yourself cheap. His desire for you is to be so aware of your purpose that even distractions bow at your presence!

Sis, I know that you hear what I am saying, but do you understand? Do you understand the power you possess?[i] Are you aware that your words can shift mountains?[ii] Did you know that you have been given the power to turn your thoughts and dreams into reality?[iii] Did anyone ever tell you that the anointing the Lord has placed on your life can rock a nation?[iv] Were you informed that you have been given weapons to dismantle the plans of the enemy, even the enemy in your mind?[v] Girl, your power is too heavy for you to misuse it! Your children, future grandchildren, and even your generation are depending on you to get it right. You cannot afford to fail. So, who are you?

Your identity can only be found in Christ. He has all the answers you are looking for. He is the only One that can define you, your purpose, and your reason for existence. Often, young men and women have asked me to show them the answer to the 'Who am I' question. Someone once said, "Mercy, it's unrealistic to say that Jesus is the only one that can give you the answer to the 'who am I' question because He is not alive." I beg to differ! He is more alive now than ever![vi] Not only is He alive, but He is available to you. He is available to answer all the questions that you might have about your existence, your life, your future, and even the smallest decisions that you want to make. All you have to do is invite Him in. Admit that you are a sinner. Surrender your life to Him and acknowledge Him as your Lord and personal Savior. Trust me! It's the best decision that you could ever make.

I know it is early in the book, but I don't think it is too early to provide you the opportunity to give your life to Christ. Give Him your life so He can reveal who you are to you. There is more to you than meets the eye, and He has the answers. You know the truth. We all want to live our best lives. We want to excel and achieve all that we can think of. Yes, we can reach all these goals. However, if we really want what God has to offer us, which is better than what our minds can fathom–we have to walk in obedience to Him. We can only do that when we give Him our lives. There is so much more to say on this topic, but I will keep it short for now. We are still coming back to this.

CHAPTER 5

The Perfect Man

I want a six-foot-tall handsome man with black hair, brown or blue eyes, has a six-pack, is rich, well-established, loves God, never lies, has five cars, a mansion, goes to church, wants to get married, and knows how to sing or play an instrument. This was the response I received from a young woman when I asked her to describe her "perfect man." I usually ask this question when someone tells me they are waiting for "the perfect man." I ask this question because it enlightens me to their level of maturity, goals, and values. Just because you are thirty-years-old doesn't mean you are ready for marriage. Age doesn't determine marriage criteria; wisdom plus several other factors do. I want you to understand that a twenty-five-year-old wise young woman may be well equipped for marriage before a thirty-five-year-old woman who has not learned the importance of commitment. Your age should not play any part in your reasoning for marriage. Marriage is beyond the number of years you have lived on earth.

Genesis 2:18 states, "Then the LORD God said, 'It is not good for the man to be alone. I will make a helper who is just right for him.'"

Let's break this scripture down. "It is NOT good for man to be alone." God was not happy with the solitude of man. I'm sure He also considered His command for man to be fruitful and to multiply. He (God) saw a need for union, and He declares it. Then He says, "I will make a helper who is just right for him." The emphasis is on the word "I." God says in the first book of the bible that He will make a helper for Adam. He didn't create Eve and then tell her to go and find Adam. He didn't tell Adam to go and look for a partner to be complete. No! He did all the necessary work. It was God's task from the beginning. It makes sense, right? I mean, the One who created you is the perfect person to match you with someone else that He created. Especially since He knows every inward part of every human He created (Psalm 139). Not only did He say He would create a helper, but He also said, "A helper who is just right for you." Wow! How awesome is God! He had already met our needs long before our creation. He didn't just pair Adam with anyone or anything; He created a partner that was just RIGHT for him. When we think about it, God could have paired Adam with an animal, and they could have been fruitful and multiplied, but God wanted to create something special for Adam. Someone that would be like him, speak like him, and act like him.

So, what are you out here looking for, Sis? Why are you searching for the man that God has already positioned for you? Did He instruct you to search? Did He give you permission to "test the waters?" I have to be honest with you so you can understand the value God has placed on your life. God did not say the woman should go out and find the man that He, the Lord, had appointed for her.

Proverbs 18:22 KJV reads, "[22]Whoso findeth a wife findeth a good thing, and obtaineth favour of the LORD."

I have to break this down to you so that you get where I am coming from. Let's look at another translation of this scripture. Proverbs 18:22 NLT, "The man who finds a wife finds a treasure, and he receives favor from the LORD."

Sis, the Lord just revealed to you that you are TREASURE! Treasure does not go looking for someone to love it; it waits patiently for the appointed person to find it. For it knows the appointed person will love and cherish it. It knows it is too beautiful to expose itself to any or everyone. It knows that the person who finds it will handle it with care.

You see, a treasure is always hidden. Many pass over the treasure without even knowing it is there. But when God appoints a person to find it, the individual begins to search for it and does not relent until he has found what he has been looking for. Now, do you understand your value? You are a valued treasure! God wants you to be hidden in Him so the right man will find you. If you expose yourself to ungodly places, blasphemous environments, shacked up with a one-night stand, doing things that are not according to the will of God for your life, there is a risk that the special person that God has assigned for you will not find you. I must say it again, God wants you to be hidden so deeply in Him, hidden in His words, hidden in His arms, because that is where your protection is. If you dwell in the secret place of the Most High under the shadow of the Almighty (Psalm 91), no one can come and snatch you up! No one can break your heart! No one can mislead you! No one can pull you out of alignment! No one can take advantage of you because you are positioned correctly. Now don't get me wrong, they will try! They will try to shift you from your position, but they will fail because you are so grounded in God.

Consider this:

Treasure hunters spend their time searching for hidden or lost treasures that may be of value in the current day and age. Whenever they go to work, they make sure they are adequately equipped with the right tools in order to be successful on their journey. They put on the proper attire for the adventure, including weighted belts, the correct headgear, comfortable shoes, and scuba equipment if they are going underwater. They carry a map and a metal detector that will guide them during the treasure hunt.

Likewise, is a man who is searching for his "rib." The man who intends to find his treasure must 1) know what he is searching for 2) know how to find this priceless jewel 3) prepare himself for the journey 4) plan out the strategies for success. For a woman who is devoted to God, the young man knows that God is the key to her heart. He knows this because he has identified that the woman he is seeking after is wrapped in the arms of her Father. Before the young man embarks on this journey, he knows he needs to find favor in the sight of her Father–so he chases after God. His initial intent may be to find the wife of his choice, but as he continues to chase after God, he falls in love with Him as well. Then, he focuses on God and allows his heart to be in the correct posture–aligned with God. I won't be surprised if you're thinking, "Man, there aren't any men like this that exist nowadays," but I beg to differ. You just need to trust God to bring Him to you.

Now, I have to be clear about something. Just because a man believes in God and goes to church does not mean he is the person who God has in store for you. Trust me, the devil is also present where the people of God are. Just because he looks like he loves Jesus, doesn't mean that he "really" loves Jesus. Or just because he loves Jesus, doesn't mean that he is the one God has chosen for you to love intimately. You have to take everything to God in prayer. Don't think for a second that your prayer is petty. There are no petty prayers, honey! If it's in your mind, bring it to the Lord in prayer. If you're thinking of doing "it," whatever the "it" is, bring it to the

Lord in prayer. If you need clarification or you're confused, bring it to the Lord in prayer.

Let me give you a few examples of how you can offer your concerns in prayer:

"Father, I need your help! You know your son ________, well he's been following me in church. I see him when he's worshipping, and he acts like he really loves you. He is always available to help people, and I know You like people like that, and let's not even begin to talk about his smile! Oh, Jesus! Okay, let's get back to the point. Lol. Jesus, I don't want to be distracted by my eyes that I fail to see your heart. What is your heart saying to me about ______, Lord? Is he the one you have sent for me, or is my flesh playing tricks on me? Jesus, tell me what you have to say concerning this matter. You have all the answer, and I am ready when You are."

Another example:

"Lord, there is this guy that really likes me at work. You know who I'm talking about. His name is ________. I like him a lot. Everything about him shouts my name. Is he the one?"

Another example:

'Thank you, Jesus, for the grace to seek You. I pray that you give me the spirit of discernment so that I will know whether this guy is the person you have purposed for me.

Please remove the lust of the flesh and guide me into your path so that I will not make a decision that will hinder, affect, or destroy my life. I give you my life and even more, in Jesus' name.

Now there are no perfect words to say, and there is no order in how you should pray. I just want to give you a kick start with the examples that I shared with you. My overall point is for you to offer every part of your life to God. He wants to know about it. Yes, He already knows about it, but He wants you to talk to Him just like you would pick up the phone to call your best friend. So, pick up your bible, get into your secret place, or just get on your knees and tell it to Jesus.

CHAPTER 6

He Still Wants You

Now don't get me wrong, if you have been in unholy environments, God can still rescue you. As a matter of fact, He wants to rescue you. He just wants you to want Him. That's all. He knows it's hard, and that's why He's asking you to choose Him. He understands the pressure that friends, society, family, and life puts on you; that's why He is ready to come to your rescue. He said that when you cry out to Him in distress, He will deliver you (Psalm 107:28). Yes, you!

I am reminded of the story of the prodigal son in Luke 15:11-32. I want to specifically point out Luke 15:20, which says, "So he returned home to his father. And while he was still a long way off, his father saw him coming. Filled with love and compassion, he ran to his son, embraced him, and kissed him." If you're not familiar with this story, here is a quick summary. There was a young man who decided that he wanted to go and live his life. He wanted to explore what the world had to offer. So, he told his dad that he wanted his portion of his dad's inheritance. The crazy thing here is that his father was still alive. The inheritance was being stored for him, and his brother so that when the time came, and his father was no longer alive, they would have some things to help them get by. Fast forward, so his dad agrees to give him his inheritance, and then the young man leaves. He spends all his money "living the life" and becomes broke. After serving as a slave to make ends meet and not being able to eat or live comfortably, the boy decides to go home. He didn't think that his father would accept him as a son anymore but was willing to be his father's servant–just so that he could survive.

Where am I going with this? Look at verse 20 again, "So he returned home to his father. And while he was still a long way off, his father saw him coming. Filled with love and compassion, he ran to his son, embraced him, and kissed him." As you can see, the father forgave his son. As a matter of fact, the father was so happy that his son returned home, as soon as he saw him coming, he RAN to his son, embraced, and kissed him.

The prodigal son thought his father had written him off because of his unwise choices, but his father understood that he was weak and immature and embraced his return. My sister, God wants to embrace your return as well. He just wants to see you coming in His direction, and He will run to you–no matter how far you have gone. He will leave the ninety-nine for you. So, take that step with faith today. He awaits you.

Back to Genesis!

Genesis 2:21-22 NLT, "So the LORD God caused the man to fall into a deep sleep. While the man slept, the LORD God took out one of the man's ribs and closed up the opening. [22] Then the LORD God made a woman from the rib, and he brought her to the man."

Let's look at a few more points here. The Lord knew Adam's needs BEFORE Adam knew His own needs. (While we are sleeping, God is handling our needs. He is at work, while we rest). When Adam fell into a deep sleep, God took out one of his ribs. Now, what's that all about? Why did God choose to remove one of the ribs? The rib encircles the chest and functions as a shelter for the lungs, heart, and other internal organs. That's amazing! The woman's function is to make sure that the husband is not empty (she must fill the position of the rib). Her function is to protect his life (the lungs), fill him with love (the heart), protect him from physical, spiritual, and emotional foreign invasions and infections (spleen), and keep him from falling apart (other internal organs).

As you can see, God has everything planned out. He already has your blueprint sketched out. He doesn't need your help in putting things in order. He did it already. It is left up to you to trust Him and trust the process He has prepared for you. The incomprehensible part of this whole journey is understanding that God has already set the date and time of when and where you will meet your future husband. He knows when the first date will happen, the proposal, the wedding, and so on. Sis, He planned it all out. He told me to remind you that BEFORE He formed you, He knew you! He set you apart for His purpose. He appointed you unto this nation (Jeremiah 1:5).

You saw me before I was born.
Every day of my life was recorded in your book.
Every moment was laid out
before a single day had passed.

Psalm 139:16 NLT.

Before we go any further, the Holy Spirit is leading me to pray for you:

"Father, I pray for your child that as she reads the lines of these pages, I pray that her heart is convicted to chase after you with every fiber in her body. I pray she is captivated by your love and experiences the embrace of your arms. I pray, dear Lord, that these words are more than just words. I pray these words will invade her and transform her into who you have called her to be. I pray, oh Lord, that she understands her value is above rubies and that she has been woven with delicacy. Remind her, Jesus, she is fearfully and wonderfully made, and you have planned her life for her. Help her to know her worth and give her the strength to be patient and to wait for you. Amen."

Okay, where were we? Oh yeah, He knew you! He knows you! He is right by your side, holding your hand as you go through this journey called life. The assurance that is revealed in Jeremiah 1:5 is life! When we understand the gravity of this verse alone, we receive freedom. God is saying that you don't have to struggle and figure this thing called life by yourself; that's what He's there for. He has your identity in His hands. Your story was written before you were formed. He called you His very own before your physical being was birthed. He has already seen your end before your beginning. Sis, you are loved! You can live in freedom now. So, stop stressing and chill.

CHAPTER 7

Addressing the Four P's

So earlier, I expressed my frustration with women rushing to the altar before they were ready. Remember the four P's purpose, power, pressure, and pleasure of marriage? Well, that's what we are going to be discussing here. I'm not going to go too deep into it, but I just want to scratch the surface.

The Purpose of Marriage.

Marriage is an institution orchestrated by God between a man and woman. But it doesn't end there. There is a purpose to the covenant of marriage. Marriage is not just about a man and woman deciding to spend the rest of their lives together. It is about displaying the image of God in human form. It is the duty of the Christian couple to present the love of God to humanity through marriage. Of all relationships that exist, marriage is the most intimate relationship that is a replica of how God wants us to love Him, and to love others. Now, as you know, many marriages do not replicate God's love. However, in all honesty, it is the closest example.

Deciding and choosing who to marry is the most crucial decision you will ever make. And, although there are do-overs, there shouldn't have to be. No one wants to do it twice! With that said, rushing into the arms of a man without being 100 percent sure is detrimental to your physical, spiritual, emotional, and mental wellbeing! Your destiny, your future, your children, and your generation depends on it! I know that seems a bit harsh, but Sis, marriage, in itself, is beyond harsh. It's not all a bed of roses, as people make it seem. It's expressing the characteristics of God whether we like it or not.

Marriage is an expression of your commitment to your husband and also to God. You don't get to run away because you don't "feel" like you're meant to be together anymore. No! It's a vow for life when you stand before God and say, "Till death do us part." Death should be the only thing that separates you and your appointed partner! That's if you are patient enough to allow God to help you choose your destiny partner. (Note: I am not referring to anyone in an abusive relationship. If you are and have tried to resolve it without success, get out! Get out of that environment. Your life matters).

As you know, the divorce rate is unspeakable, and the divorce rate amongst Christians has also increased. This should not be the case. We have to get it right! Now, I didn't say that the man that you will marry will be perfect; the perfect man doesn't exist. We are all imperfect people. God joins two imperfect people and creates perfection in His eyes. Emphasis on His eyes! Don't get excited just yet. God doesn't do all the work for us. He helps us through, but He requires our effort. There is no sitting back and waiting for help to fall from the sky. You have to do the work.

The Power of Marriage.

The union of a man and a woman is the union of power. Whether negative or positive, the two merge forces and produce power. What is even more alarming is that marrying the wrong person is powerful enough to alter destinies. When married to the right person, you can grow, create, laugh, and cry together. You can produce things that seem impossible to the human eye. However, marriage to the wrong person can destroy so many things, from the self to the seed. Let me explain. When you marry the wrong person, it can cause you to do things you wouldn't have ever imagined doing before. Marriage to the wrong person can make you depressed, isolated, and lonely. Marriage has the power to turn a happy person into a sad person and vice versa. It can take someone who had a lot of goals and potential and make them end up being a drug addict or a murderer. Marriage is powerful. Marriage can also affect the seed. The seed is anything birthed together from the union of the two individuals. This includes businesses, the physical home, children, and anything else created together.

The power within a union should never be underestimated. Trust me, when two individuals realize the power of their union, they can rock a nation. BUT it has to be with the right person. That person will see your ability and encourage you to reach for the sky. He will not be intimidated by your strengths. He is a king who will know his place in his castle and be willing to step off his throne to help his queen. He speaks well of her. He loves her. He motivates her. He knows his power, and he uses it to empower her.

The Pressure of Marriage.

When you leave the single status and join the married community, there is so much joy to be experienced. You no longer have to "do life" by yourself. You now have a teammate, and that teammate is for life! What an honor it is that God gives to us, but with marriage comes pressure. There is pressure on the side of the husband and the wife. The husband realizes he is now responsible for a household. He must give up his selfish ways and consider the needs of someone else. He must realize he is the provider for his family. He must attend to his wife's physical and emotional needs. He must provide a safe haven for his family. His focus is on his family. He is a dad, a friend, a disciplinarian, and a role model. He is a partner, a supporter, a decision-maker, and a leader; the pressure he endures is endless.

Another major pressure that a man must endure is with his emotions. Most men refuse to express their emotions about the things they are going through. They have to be strong for their family; they cannot allow their weakness to overcome them. That's got to be so hard! Imagine! I couldn't do it! I would lose my sanity! I guess that's why God made me a woman. Lol. The husband is the knight to the damsel. He has a truckload full of duties. Yikes!

For the woman, in addition to the load of the husband (which is equally hers), her load is mighty. She is no longer just a damsel. she is also a mother, a cook, a creator, homemaker, friend, nurturer, lover, provider, partner, wife, nurse, co-provider, prayer warrior, and helper. To be honest, her list is unlimited. Have you read Proverbs 31? Girl, that's a checklist that she strives to attain. She's superwoman, alright! Whew! Imagine the pressure that comes with such a huge responsibility. It's not for the faint at heart. The reward is beautiful, but the pressure is only for those who are ready to take on the role. Be mindful, these roles should not and cannot be neglected.

The Pleasure of Marriage.

Grab a cup of coffee and take a seat, Sis. This one requires your ultimate attention! Everyone knows that marriage is a beautiful thing, and that is why almost everyone wants to experience it. I mean, who wouldn't want to experience happiness, satisfaction, enjoyment, and fulfillment? It is such an amazing feeling to be and feel loved.

Sex is one of the pleasures in marriage, and every damsel that I have mentored or counseled has asked me about it. I have to be totally honest with you; I had questions about it too. There are very few who want to wait to be married in order to enjoy the sexual pleasures of marriage. Some of the reasons I get vary from, "I don't want to be inexperienced." "I'm afraid that I won't know what to do." "I want to try different men out before I settle down." "I want to have fun."

My response to these women usually starts with, "After marriage, you can enjoy all the sex you want, but until then, patience is the key."

God knew that we would need to be intimate, and that's why He created a capsule for it. Listen, God wants you to have sex, but not with any and everyone. Remember that you are the model of Christ; you are emulating the image of God. Loyalty is one of the characteristics that God possesses, and you ought to possess the same characteristic. Before marriage, your body belongs to God, and after marriage, He allows you to share your body with your partner. Sex is a powerful tool. It joins two individuals into one. There is an exchange of heightened emotions, spirituality, and the physical aspect of fluid. Your spouse becomes a part of you for life. Yes, girl, for life! Even if protection is used, some transfer will still occur, and that's why most contraceptives say that you are ninety-nine percent protected. Honey, there is still that one percent lingering!

I have hosted seminars on purity and sex. During one session, I had a panel of guests. The panel included the married couple, the single person, the engaged, and the divorced couple. Those who participated in pre-marital sexual intercourse all agreed that if they were to see someone they had previously dated and were intimate with, they would remember every detail that transpired between the two. If they could do it all over again, ninety-nine percent agreed they would wait for their "Mr. Right." I remember one young lady exclaiming, "What was I thinking?" When the flesh is in charge, we often forget to think; we go with our emotions. Baby girl, you have too much to risk! You are priceless, and so is your body. The pleasure of sex can wait for marriage.

Let's deal with the spiritual transfer for a moment. When you engage in sexual intercourse before marriage, there is also a lifetime connection that is formed. Souls are tied. Hearts are touched, and an unerasable attachment is created. Imagine creating that with someone who will not be your husband! Your soul will experience distraction, whether positive or negative, whenever you see your previous sex partner. If you end up marrying someone who does not meet the standards of your previous partner, you will have sexual desires that will affect your emotions, your desires, and your marriage. Your husband will never be enough for you. Also, there is a strong possibility that you will venture outside of your marriage to meet your sexual needs. That is a struggle in itself. So why rush?

God knew all of this, and that is why He created sex for marriage. It has to stay within the marriage. When a husband and wife join in sexual intercourse, it can be seen as a form of worship. They explore and embrace one another. They show deep intimate love towards each other. This type of intimacy is not for the guy around the corner who just wants to test drive you. Nah, sis, you are not cheap. You are authentic! The real deal! And your worth, (say it with me), "Is beyond rubies!" If he wants you, he can wait for you! If he wants you, he will honor you and your values! If he wants you, he will chase after the One that owns you! So, he wants to show you how much he loves you, right? Tell him that he can do that by respecting your boundaries. That is love. When he shows you that he will do anything to have you, including wait, that is love. Remember, sister, the pressure is real, so don't pressurize yourself into something before the right time.

So, there you have it! The purpose, power, pressure, and pleasure of marriage. Now I just scratched the surface of these topics, and this is not the end. We will be discussing this in more depth in one of my other volumes–stay tuned. Nevertheless, I want you to be encouraged. You will experience all of the beautiful things in marriage; but, wait on it so that it will be a once-in-a-lifetime experience. I'm rooting for you, girl.

CHAPTER 8

Distractions

Sister girl, where is your mind? What are you thinking about? What's keeping you up at night and controlling your thoughts? Why haven't you started that business venture that you keep thinking about? Why aren't you writing down those amazing ideas that keep lingering in your mind? What's keeping you from writing and publishing your first book? Why is that application sitting on the table? What's your excuse for not looking into repairing your credit? Why have you refused to apply to that school? Why are you distracted?

It's crazy how we all have a million and one things to do, and we can barely get one out of the way! I know this feeling all too well. I recently went through this phase where I wanted to do so many things, but when I looked back, I barely got anything done. I was so frustrated with myself. I knew what I had to do, but I just couldn't get it done, and for the life of me, I couldn't figure out why. This book is a perfect example.

God gave me the vision for this book in 2017. The insane thing about it is that God gave me step-by-step directions! He gave me the name of the book, how it should be structured, and all. I started writing, and I was so overwhelmed by the Holy Spirit that my fingers wouldn't stop moving. I remember the exact time and place for this vision. I was sitting in my office in my clinic. It was 4:32 pm, and God just started to speak to me. He said, "Write what I am saying. I picked up my pen, and I began to write. By the time I was done writing, I had the first page filled. After I was finished with the first page, He then began to give me instructions on how He wanted this book to look and those to come. Girl, I tell you, by the time I was done, I saw at least ten books, and this is just for the first portion! I said to myself, "I can't do this! This is impossible!"

He responded to me, "I will do it through you."

Girl, I wanted to leap and shout and scream and dance! I had never been so confident of the voice that I was hearing and the One speaking those words. I just knew that it was a move of God. Instantly, I called my goddaughter, Sarah, and said, "Sit down and listen to this." I read the first page. She was on the edge of her seat and could barely stay still. She was like, what just happened to you–this is amazing. I was so overwhelmed that I didn't know what to say, so I kept silent. Then God gave me more inspiration to write, and I did.

Before I knew it, a patient came in. I stopped and attended to my patient. Once her visit was complete, I sent her on her merry way. I hurried back into my office to keep writing, but my cellphone rang. My husband was calling me. "Babe, where are you? It's 7 o'clock." I didn't even realize that much time had passed. I usually close up at 6:00 p.m.

Sarah hadn't even bothered to stop me. I asked her why and she said, "I could see you were on another level; I didn't want to be the one that would mess that up." I smiled and quickly packed up my things and hurried to my car so I could get home.

After arriving home, I started attending to the needs of my children and husband. Later, I decided to pick up my laptop to write a bit more. I wrote two lines, and then all I could hear was, "Mum!!!" I got up and assisted my oldest daughter, who needed help finding something in the game room. After helping her, I prayed with the children and sent them to bed.

Finally, peace and quiet, or so I thought. I settled in my bed, opened my laptop, put my fingers on the keyboard, and then my one-year-old flung open the door and ran to my bed. I realized nothing would get done that night, so I decided to put my laptop away and put my baby, Joseph, to sleep. I ended up falling asleep, too.

Days went by. I could barely write all that was laid on my heart. I did most of my work at night after the kids went to sleep, but I was so exhausted from work and motherhood, I really didn't do much. Fast forward to six months later, and the book was not complete. I did write, but it wasn't as much as I wanted to. I was so distracted with being a mother, a wife, a sister, a mentor, a family nurse practitioner, a business-woman, a youth minister, and the list goes on. By the time I looked at my book, I hadn't accomplished much. What was I doing? I quickly realized I had not prioritized my goals. I was doing things as they came, and I could scarcely complete one assignment. I was distracted!

Why am I telling you this? Because the life of a wife, mother, or anyone with a number of responsibilities is busy. Balancing my relationship with God was also a challenge. Sometimes I was hot, while other times I was cold. Some days I picked up my bible, and other days I was so tired that I couldn't find the strength to pick it up. My Christian life and my relationship with God were suffering. I'm sure you know that if you are too busy to fit God into your schedule, you are busy not doing what He has instructed you to do. I had to make it right. I changed up what I was doing. I organized myself and put my priorities in order. At the top of my list was and still is my relationship with God.

"I want you to be free from the concerns of this life. An unmarried man can spend his time doing the Lord's work and thinking about how to please him. But a married man has to think about his earthly responsibilities and how to please his wife.

His interests are divided. In the same way, a woman who is no longer married or has never been married can be devoted to the Lord and holy in body and in spirit.

But a married woman has to think about her earthly responsibilities and how to please her husband. I am saying this for your benefit, not to place restrictions on you. I want you to do whatever will help you serve the Lord best, with as few distractions as possible." [vii]

These are the words of Paul the Apostle to the people of Corinth. As one with many responsibilities, I can understand why Paul said these words, and I couldn't agree any less with him.

I know marriage looks like a beautiful adventure, and honey, it is, but you can do so much more in your singleness. I often tell my single sisters, "Reach for every height attainable and those that are not attainable, reach for those, too, while you are still single." It's not that success cannot be done while you are married, but when you are without a husband, children, and all the other responsibilities that come with marriage, you can reach for the sky without looking back. Lol.

Sis, do all that you can while you are single. Work with every fiber in your being for God and store up those treasures in heaven. I need you to find your identity in Christ before you decide to add anyone else on your journey called life. Pray to God and find out what His design for your life looks like. Ask Him questions and follow His lead. Do not, and I repeat, do not try to answer those questions by yourself. Go on your knees in prayer and let God lead you. Become intimate with God by developing your relationship with Him through His Word, prayer, and worship. Do everything you can to improve your relationship with Him. Explore all that God has in store for you. Be equally yoked. Embrace your belief in God. Go to school. Get educated. Read books. Go to conferences. Sail the world. Impact others. Give to your neighbor. Be a helping hand. A shoulder to cry on. Help a friend in need. Let Christ reflect in your daily living. Refuse to be controlled by the world; instead, allow the Holy Spirit to guide your every step. Work like there's no tomorrow. Live every day like it's your last, and you will be visiting the King once you close your eyes to sleep. Most especially show love, be love, and live in love. Don't let anyone take advantage of you. Secure what is yours and do your best. Work for God, Sis, make Him proud. Live your single life to the fullest and pray while you are at it. Trust me, God will bring your prince charming to you at the right time.

Also, don't allow the cares of this world to distract you. Don't allow men who don't even know what they want for their lives to divert your attention from what is important. Refuse to accept less than the best because you deserve it. You are the daughter of the King. Life in itself is distracting. We are even introduced to certain people in the bible who were distracted. One story that comes to my mind is about

Martha and Mary. Let me give you a quick overview. Jesus came to visit Mary and Martha. Martha (rightfully so) decided to prepare food for Jesus to eat. While Martha was working hard in the kitchen, Mary sat close to Jesus' feet and listened while He taught. Martha was not happy about Mary's straight disregard for not helping with dinner. She complained to Jesus, and Jesus said, "*My dear Martha, you are worried and upset over all these details! There is only one thing worth being concerned about. Mary has discovered it, and it will not be taken away from her.*"[viii] Whoa, that was not the response Martha was expecting. I'm sure she was convinced that Jesus was going to say something like, "Mary, you need to get up, go to the kitchen, and help your sister," but she was wrong.

You see, Martha wasn't doing anything wrong. She was prepping a delicious meal for Jesus, but there was something even more important than that. The food of the soul. Mary's heart was hungry for the everlasting meal, and nothing was going to stop her from getting it. Maybe she knew they weren't going to have Jesus forever, and she made sure she took advantage of every moment possible with the Lord.

Beautiful Damsel, this is exactly what God wants you to do. He wants you to be hungry for Him and to seek after the food of heaven. He wants you to take the "Mary position" and soak in all that He has to tell you. Your friends can wait. The laundry can wait. Your boyfriend can wait. It's too early for you to be distracted. You have so much awaiting you.

What matters is that you open your heart to receive while you are still able. So, sit down at the feet of Jesus and soak it all in. Don't be distracted by the minor things in life. I will say it again, store up your treasures in heaven.

I want you to put this book down and go on your knees in prayer. Although I would love for you to finish this book in one sitting, there is something more important, and that is your connection with God. He needs your attention more than anything in this world, including this book. Get in your "Mary position" and pray. Ask God for counsel. Ask Him for direction. Cry your eyes out to Him. Confess that you have been so distracted that you didn't even remember to add Him to your schedule. Be honest and open with Him. I promise you He won't disown you. He won't throw you away. As a matter of fact, when you are open and honest with Him, He will securely wrap His arms around you and give you peace. Let Him in on the secrets that you wouldn't dare tell your friend. He's waiting!

CHAPTER 9

When Will It Be My Turn?

You're back! Awesome. Let's continue.

A young lady called me. I had never spoken to or seen her before. She said that she got my number from someone mutual. She stated she needed someone to talk to and that some young adults had recommended me. "I've been feeling so meaningless. I am thirty-two-years-old, and I haven't accomplished anything." She started to cry. I listened. She continued, "I don't see the point in even living. I wake up every day feeling numb to the world. I am just existing. All my friends are married, and I'm always the one singled out. Most of them have children already and are so happy." She paused and then said, "I don't know why I feel this way, but I just do. I feel worthless." I asked her to tell me the scenario around when she began to feel so beat down. She confessed that it was after the summer of 2015. Three of her friends had just gotten married, and she was the maid of honor at one and a bridesmaid at the other two. She told me she was so happy for them that she danced the night away.

However, deep down inside, she was jealous, angry, and frustrated.

After she was done venting, I began to ask questions to get insight into her background. Here's what I found out, Jasmine (not her real name) was thirty-two-years-old, an engineer who works in a well-known oil and gas company. She held a managerial position in that company and was doing extremely well. She also co-hosted a small group class once a month with one of her friends who was married. Jasmine had so much going for her, but she didn't realize it because she was so focused on where she thought she should be by the age of thirty-two. All the achievements listed above seemed minor compared to getting married and having children. She wanted to be on the same level as her friends. Without the title of "wife" and "mother," she felt she hadn't achieved it. You see, Jasmine was so consumed with everyone else's season that she didn't take the time to assess her own.

Sound familiar? Are you coveting someone else's life? Are you wishing for your friend's life? Honey, stop and look at what God has given you. Your life isn't as bad as it seems. You are doing things! Listen, a tree doesn't grow overnight. It must be planted, watered, and cared for. You are in your planting season, baby. God is watching, preparing, and watering you for the right time. Embrace your "now." Your "now" is so important. Many people overlook the "now" season because they feel that those who are experiencing it are immature and inexperienced. Your time is now. Now is the time to see where the Lord has placed you. Now is the time for you to operate in this season. It's your turn to realize that God is positioning you for something great. It's your turn to soak yourself in the presence of your Maker so that He can fill you up with everything you need. It's your turn to ignore the enemy with every word of failure he speaks into your ear. It's your turn to receive the treasures awaiting you now. It's your turn to conquer this season the Lord has blessed you with. It's your turn to prove to the enemy that his words mean nothing compared to the plans the Lord has for your life. You can't ignore your "now" season. You can't sleep in your "now" season. You have to get up! You have to act! Your time is now!!!

I remember a statement from an elderly lady at my church. She said, "I wish I would have remembered the Lord in my youth." She continued, "If I knew then what I know now, I would have done things a whole lot different." I was perplexed at her statement. Why was she regretting her life as a child? Couldn't she do what she wanted to do then, now? I was probably around fourteen-years-old when I listened to her speak. I held onto those words. Sometime later, I came across this scripture, and it all clicked.

"Don't let the excitement of youth cause you to forget your Creator. Honor Him in your youth before you grow old and say, "Life is not pleasant anymore..."

Remember Him before your legs–the guards of your house-start to tremble; and before your shoulders-the strong men-stoop...

Remember Him before the door to life's opportunities is closed and the sound of work fades.

Remember Him before you become fearful of falling and worry about danger in the streets; before your hair turns white like an almond tree in bloom, and you drag along without energy like a drying grasshopper...Remember Him before you near the grave, your everlasting home, when the mourners will weep at your funeral."[ix]

So, what did the elderly woman mean by her statement? She realized the importance of Singleness. Singleness is a gift from God, but very few realize it. In your singleness season, see it as an opportunity to get to know, date, and marry Jesus. God does so much developing in this season. He uses the single-season to plant and water each individual. He doesn't just shift you from one season to the next; He makes sure that the young woman is ready for the next stage. How sweet it is of God to care so much about His creation. I remember telling a young lady that "God would never throw you into the ocean and then leave you to find your way back to shore." No! He is not like that. If you find yourself in the ocean, trust that He is there to take you to shore. As a matter of fact, He is the water surrounding you. He is your flotation device. He will never let you drown. He will never let you down. He will never leave you.

CHAPTER 10

Tune In To Your Now

If we would all understand the "NOW" concept, life would be much easier. We chase after our future and fail to realize that what we are looking for is within us. It is not ahead of us. All we need to do is search within, and we will find the future that we are looking for. The experiences, challenges, and obstacles we go through in life are all necessary when searching for our mysterious future. As we mature, we realize why God places us in different seasons. Different seasons yield growth. Different seasons reveal new opportunities, and each season is a training field. We need the seasons for growth. We cannot rush growth. A four-month-old infant who sees his sister running may try to stand up to run but will inadvertently fall, not because he doesn't have the determination, but because it's not yet time. He still needs to learn how to sit and crawl properly. He needs to allow his bones to build stamina. He needs to learn how to stand and balance. He needs to learn how to walk first. He may not be running now, but once his season is ripe, he will take off, and nothing will stop him. The same concept goes for you, sis. You may see others at the finish line, and you feel like you are yet to begin, but I want you to trust the process and embrace your learning season.

What are you doing now? How can you embrace your "now?" How can you tune in to your now? So, you are single, right? And God hasn't revealed Mr. Right for you. Life isn't over! Honey, it just started! You need to focus on yourself. If you are in school, use this time to focus on school and be all that you can be. Don't just pass the class, ACE the class! Master the art of your degree. Find places where you can give back and volunteer there. Look for internships that are related to your degree and apply for them.

For my high school sisters, use your free time to look for scholarships that can help you on your journey in college. Check out companies like Walmart, Coca-Cola, AISES, Google, McDonald's, Chevron, Microsoft, and Generation google scholarship (to name a few). Look into small and big companies and do your research to find out if they provide scholarships or grants. If you're in college, do this as well. Everyone needs help, and there are plenty of resources that can help.

To all of my sisters who are fresh out of university and haven't been hired yet, don't give up! Keep on sending those applications out. If you really want to work in a specific place, pray about it, and if God is leading you to work there,

He will make a way. Volunteer there, start low if you have to, but be persistent. Don't let someone's "no" kill your drive! But while applying for your dream job, apply at other companies as well. God might want to use you in a different place for a bigger testimony. Don't let money be your driving force! Let the Holy Spirit and your passion (which should be in tune with the Holy Spirit) steer the wheel for you. Every time you get knocked down, stand with more force and determination to reach your dreams.

God didn't forget about you, yes honey, you! I know you're frustrated at your place of employment right now, but that isn't a reason to quit. The steps that lead to your next level are called patience.

James 1:12 NLT

"God blesses those who patiently endure testing and temptation. Afterward they will receive the crown of life that God has promised to those who love Him."

Take note. Life in itself is a journey of patience. When we rush, we end up stumbling, and a lot of times, we end up in trouble. Don't rush to quit that job, instead pray about it and ask God for direction. Ask Him to open up your heart so that you can be sensitive to His voice, His instruction, and His teaching. Ask God to show you what He wants you to learn during this season. Ask Him to reveal to you how you can be in tune and active in your current season. I know it's hard, but you cannot make a move without God's direction, or you will just end up at another job that will frustrate you even further. God wants you to learn patience and the beauty of patience. I have realized that when I am patient, I enjoy what God gives me more than when I rush. What is God giving you in this season at your place of employment? There is beauty in every situation, so start to list the things that can be viewed as beautiful. It's easier said than done, but it can be done. Even the things or people that make life frustrating at work can be viewed as beautiful.

CHAPTER 11

Embrace Your Now

Are you working in a fast-food restaurant while you go to school, and you are tired of flipping burgers? Look at the customers that come in and see the beauty in them. God created them for a purpose. Everyone holds a lesson for another to learn from. Look at the place where you work. God has given you the privilege to be able to work and support yourself. Thank God that you are not on the street begging for food. Even those on the street are thanking God they are above the ground and not beneath. Thank God for the friends you have made at work and even the enemies. It's all a lesson in life. Imagine what you could learn from where you are currently working. You might become a business owner in the future. God is teaching you how to manage those above and beneath you.

Are you working as a certified nurse assistant in a local hospital? Sister girl, you have so much to be thankful for, and there is so much beauty in your lenses. Give thanks for every patient that comes and leaves alive because you had something to do with that. Even if the patient was not in your direct care, you are a part of the team, and that is beautiful. Look at the patients that you are caring for? Give thanks that you are not being cared for in a hospital. Rather you are being used as an instrument to care for others. When you walk into a patient's room, smile and give thanks to God that you are being used as a vessel to serve others. Every time you complete a task, see the beauty in it and give thanks that God saw you through. Find the beauty in every breath you breathe. Remember, there are some patients who need an oxygen tank to help them breathe. Every step you take is a testimony. Some are not as fortunate, and they are thanking God for the grace to move around.

To the young lady who hasn't found a job yet and the one who was terminated from her place of employment, it's going to be okay. I promise that God knows every single thing that you are going through right now, and He has a reason and purpose for it. You may not understand, but remember that He said, in Isaiah 55:8-9 NLT[x] "*My thoughts are nothing like your thoughts, and my ways are far beyond anything you could imagine. For just as the heavens are higher than the earth, so My ways are higher than your ways and My thoughts higher than your thoughts.*"

You will not always understand why you are going through a certain thing, but I want you to trust that God does, and that is all that matters. So, while you are in your waiting season, don't just sit there. Like I said before, keep filling out those applications and use this as a time to build yourself. Find your calling. Do you like to speak publicly? Build yourself up with online classes. Look into certifications in your desired field. Do you want to impact a specific population? Research your target market and see how you can be a vessel. Do you love helping others? Commit to serving an hour or two, or even more if you so desire, at a food bank or pantry. Are you a prayer warrior? Start to build yourself and others up in prayer in your closet. If God is asking you to go further, you can start a prayer conference line, a prayer group at your home or in your community. Do you desire to spread the word of God, and you are not shy? Find legal locations where you can stand outside and evangelize to lost souls. Are you into fashion? Research and see how you can turn your passion into a ministry. Partner with small companies, learn from them, and build your own.

So, you can dance really well, and you love kids. Try to see how you can get involved in an after-school program to teach little kids how to dance. You're a single sister, and you love cooking. Create an event at home where you can invite other single sisters and teach them how to make various dishes. Invite those who are engaged and married as well. Are you interested in sewing? Go on YouTube and start from the basics. Learn how to thread a needle and go from there. You can learn to sew teddy bears for your local hospital and donate them to the Neonatal Intensive Care Unit. Trust me, the parents will appreciate it, and you will put a smile on someone's face. Do you like doing hair? Learn how to make hair for those who are suffering from cancer or alopecia. You're a math whiz, right? Check out your local elementary schools and find out how you can be of use to students who are struggling in class. You can even be a tutor in your community. All you have to do is open your PowerPoint, create a flyer, and then post it around your community. Girl, someone needs help somewhere.

Are you at every restaurant tasting new foods? Find out how you can be a food taster or start a blog and write your reviews on the restaurants where you eat. Hey, computer genius! Everyone needs to know what you're capable of! Stop hiding your talent. Build yourself with online classes and create something out of what you have learned. Go to non-profit organizations, help them out and then go further and sell your skills. Everyone wants to be tech-savvy; you might just be the key. Are you an exercise guru? Start free classes in your community and help your community lose weight and be healthy. You love to sing, but you don't want too much attention. Listen, nursing homes, shelters, and orphanages love it when people come and volunteer their time and their voices. I didn't forget about my writers out there. Put your thoughts on paper or the computer, and turn it into a book, a comic, a magazine. Write poems, journals, just get to writing. Artists!!! It's your turn. You have the talent; now start putting it to use. Create paintings that tell a story and then sell them. Use platforms like eBay, Amazon, Pinterest, Craigslist, and Offer Up.

I am addicted to stationery supplies, and I love collecting them. If you're a stationery fanatic, you can put your love to good use. Learn how to create the stationery that you love but with your signature touch on it. Your signature might be quotes, bible verses, inspirational messages, etc. Whatever it is, add it to your design, create stationery with a twist, and sell your merchandise. Now, I'm not saying go out there and do just anything. I'm saying figure out what you love to do. The thing that keeps you up at night. Take the idea that makes your heart full of passion, and work on those things.

I know you think you're not qualified, and you won't be successful in that area, but do it anyway. I bet David would have laughed at the idea that one day he would be a King. I'm sure he would have been in disbelief if he was told that people would read about and emulate his behaviors thousands of years later. I'm sure Elijah from Tishbe would have rejected the thought that because of his fierce confidence in front of Jezebel on Mount Carmel, thousands would dare to stand and fight every spiritual and physical enemy that comes in the form of cancer, poverty, shame, failure, and the list goes on. It is because of the evidence of Moses' work and faith as he parted the Red Sea that has caused millions to believe that if they call upon the name of the Lord, He will save them! Abraham had no idea that his faith in following God's directive to leave his homeland would be a stepping-stone that others would look upon and trust God. With all of his efforts, Noah probably had no idea that his faith, obedience, dedication, and perseverance would impact generations to come. He would be in such disbelief if given the privilege to see how his existence transformed millions.

I can list hundreds of people in and out of the Bible who dared to look beyond the fact that they lacked wisdom, power, fame, courage, financial ability, strength, and influence. However, they trusted God to work through them. Honey, your calling is beyond you, but it is also inside of you. You have to tap into every talent that is buried within you and build upon it. Everything you will become is already within you. Now search for it, for you do not know which will yield fruit. Don't be idle. Idle people allow themselves to become prey to Satan and his tactics.

I love what Solomon said in the book of Ecclesiastes, "*Just as you cannot understand the path of the wind or the mystery of a tiny baby growing in its mother's womb, so you cannot understand the activity of God, who does all things. Plant your seed in the morning and keep busy all afternoon, for you don't know if profit will come from one activity or another–or maybe both.*"[xi]

Therefore, work in expectation that all that you do will yield positive fruit.

CHAPTER 12

Calling

Now, I know I touched on this previously, but I must shed a little more light on the very reason for our existence due to its importance. We all have the same ultimate purpose, but God has called us to different assignments. Your assignment takes many forms. Your calling or vocation is one of your assignments given to you by God. It is also your calling that leads you to your purpose.

I have encountered many people who search diligently for their calling with the right and the wrong intentions. We must understand that our calling is not to intimidate, boast, or make others feel inferior. The sole purpose of our calling is to fulfill the assignment that God has given us on earth. But know this: the answer resides only in the hands of the Lord. Before you decide to choose a calling, seek God first. Before we explore our purpose, we must visit the Creator first. I love what Paul said in 1 Corinthians 2:6-10 MSG version. He said:

"God's wisdom is something mysterious that goes deep into the interior of His purposes. You don't find it lying around on the surface. It's not the latest message, but more like the oldest–what God determined as the way to bring out His best in us, long before we ever arrived on the scene. The experts of our day haven't a clue about what this eternal plan is...No one's ever seen or heard anything like this, Never so much as imagined anything quite like it–what God has arranged for those who love him."[xii]

You see, God wants to bring out the best in us. This was His plan all along. His plan has never been less than the best. So, we need Him to determine who and what we should be. I have had so many people come to me and ask what their purpose or calling is. I always direct them to God. I pray with them and speak as the Lord compels me to. I tell them what I know they are good at and where I see their passion, but I always send them right back to God. He is the manufacturer, right? So, He gets the first and final say. He knows who He designed every single person to be. Therefore, you and I must seek Him so that He can answer our questions.

Another one of my favorite scriptures is Ephesians 1:4-5. I love this scripture because it reminds me that God already had me in mind before I even existed. Imagine that! The Creator of the entire universe ALREADY thought about you BEFORE He created you. There is power in these two verses. That means that He didn't just create you just because He thought about you. He thought about who you would be, what you would become, how you would live, who you would impact, the way He would pull you through, the life you would live, and everything you could possibly imagine. He thought about it! He thought about you! He planned out your life before you were conceived. He imagined every step before He got to work in you. Sis! He created you so He could love you. So, whatever it is He has called you to, He knows it, and He can tell you. I love what Ephesians 1:11-12 says in the same scripture:

"It's in Christ that we find out who we are and what we are living for. Long before we first heard of Christ and got our hopes up, he had His eye on us, had designs on us for glorious living, part of the overall purpose he is working out in everything and everyone."[xiii]

What an assurance! Wait, sis! Did you hear that? I know you read it, but did you hear it? Go back and read it out loud again! It is in Christ that we find out who we are and what we are living for! In Christ! Not in our desires, not in the words of another, not even in our passion! The answer resides in Christ, and not only are we living, but He designed us for glorious living! Abundant living! (That's another book on its own). The truth is if you want to know what He has called you to do and be–you must go to Him! We must soak ourselves in His Words. That is where the answers lie. Refuse to live by the speculations of others. He has the answer. Remember, there is a purpose in your existence.

Beware of Comparison When Searching for Your Calling

Comparison is a destroyer of destiny. You will never feel complete with comparisons. Once you have accomplished one standard, you will reach for the next. There is no satisfaction in comparison. We have all done it before. Yes, admit it. We have all compared ourselves to one person or the other. Especially as a damsel, a comparison is almost inevitable. Think about it. How did comparison make you feel? Yes, you may have found pleasure in realizing that you were better than someone in one aspect. But what if the person you compared yourself to was above you? How would it make you feel? Not so good, I bet! It's time to realize that comparison is like digging a pit for yourself and then burying yourself with your own hands. With no help, you pull yourself down. You search for and create flaws and use your imagination to create ideations that you are less than what you really are. If not controlled, comparison can be the beginning of one's downfall.

So, I want to urge you today, sis, to focus on you. Yes, I have said this before, and I will continue to stress it. Do not walk in the shadow of your sister with the desire to be her, or you will lose sight of who God has called you to be. I don't know about you, but one thing that I fear the most is that I will leave the earth with the things God placed inside me. The things that He instructed me to leave on earth. I don't want to do that. I want to leave empty! I want to be so emptied that there is nothing left within me other than my spirit.

I want to be able to return to the Father and show Him that I gave it my all. I left no stone unturned. I want to use all of my efforts to pour into the world He created me to be in. I want you to do the same, Sis.

I want you to understand the urgency of your mission. You don't know when you'll take your last breath, so live like it is now! Live like your last breath is tomorrow! Live like you do not have any time left. My goal is not to scare you. I don't want you to be afraid, but I do want you to realize that the things God has placed deep down on the inside of you needs to come out now! I don't want anything to hold you back. I don't want anything to stop you. I want you to be strong in the Lord and in the power of His might! I want you to put on the whole armor of God. I want you to realize who you are and walk in that anointing.

You have been called! You have been chosen for such a time as this. Now is your time. Now is the season that God has prepared for you. Satan has held you back for way too long; the shackles are breaking right now!

Satan, your time is up! Get your hands off of my sister! You are no longer welcome in her heart, her mind, her soul, or her spirit! Take your bags and get to stepping! Get out of her room, get out of her house, get out of her school, get out of her career! Pack your bags and leave! She resists you today; therefore, you must flee from her (James 4:7). We declare these things in the name of Jesus, get out! Everyone bows to the name of Jesus because at the name of Jesus EVERY knee must bow, and EVERY tongue must confess that Jesus is the Lord (Philippians 2:10-11) because His name is exalted higher than every other name. The name of Jesus is superior to every other name, so I command you today to let go of my sister! Get out of her life! Be gone!

Wooh! He's gone, sis!

Praise break!!!!

Alright, let's get down to business! The enemy isn't here. We have things to discuss. But, wait! Before I continue, I have to tell you something. Come closer, listen to me. We just drove the enemy out, but that doesn't mean the fight is over. Now we have to go harder! Understand that the Word says, "*When the unclean spirit has gone out of a person, it passes through waterless places seeking rest, but finds none. Then it says, 'I will return to my house from which I came.' And when it comes, it finds the house empty, swept, and put in order. Then it goes and brings with it seven other spirits more evil than itself, and they enter and dwell there...*"[xiv]. Why am I telling you this? Because I need you to be on fire for God! I need you to replace that empty space with the word of God. If you replace that space with the Word, the enemy will not have the opportunity to come back because there will be no more room for him. So, what do you have to do? Trust in God. Surrender your entire being to Him. Pray! Read the word of God and apply it to your life. You have to do this to successfully walk in your purpose. Let's get a little deeper.

CHAPTER 13

Trust In God

I want to share the story of someone I met a few years ago. A young lady, twenty-two years old, who was a very busy person, was always doing something. One day I got a text from her. She said she wanted to have a word with me. I asked her if everything was okay, and she said yes. I was surprised because Natasha never had time to stop and chat. Anyway, she scheduled a date with me and promised to be there. On the day we were scheduled to meet, I sat at Starbucks waiting for her. Ten minutes went by, then twenty, and then thirty-five minutes. I texted her several times to let her know I was waiting for her. When she didn't show up, I got up and made my way to my car.

Outside, I began looking in my bag, searching for my keys. I had a sudden urge to look up. As I looked up, I saw Natasha sitting in her car. I saw a tear stream down her face. I walked over to the car, and she looked up. Without exchanging any words, I walked over to the passenger's side of her car. I opened the door and took a seat. No words, just silence. A few minutes later, with faint words, she began to speak.

"I am so sorry I kept you waiting. I saw you when you drove into Starbucks, but I couldn't muster up the courage to come to you. I saw every text that you sent me, but I didn't know how to respond. I just don't know where to start. I am so lost, so confused. I don't know what is going on in my life. I thought being a Christian was supposed to be easier than this. I don't know why it is so hard. I don't understand why everyone else is making it, and I am barely surviving. I feel like I'm drowning. I have so many friends who don't believe in God, and they are making it. They don't go to church as much as I do. They don't serve in a church. They just live life, and they're making it. How come it's not working for me? What am I doing wrong? I make sure that I am always doing something, but I don't seem to see the reward of my hard work. I have everything under control, but yet nothing is working! Why? Why don't things work out in my favor? Why is God so angry with me? What have I done for God to turn a deaf ear to me? What have I done? I can't seem to catch a breath. I need help."

We spoke for a long time. After quite a bit of questions, I found out that Natasha lost her best friend, Jennifer, three years ago. She had suffered from a brain tumor. Prior to her death, part of the tumor had been removed. She was with Jennifer every step of the way. They prayed together every day. She was so sure that her best friend would be ok. She professed scriptures citing promises of life and not death over her, but soon after, she received the news that her friend passed away. A few days before her friend died, she realized that Jennifer had not given her life to Christ. She missed the opportunity to share Jesus with her, and this played on her mind constantly.

The following year, she found out that she was not accepted into the medical program she applied for. Natasha was drained. She was losing hope. She felt like God had left her. She thought that God was angry with her. She was exhausted carrying all this weight on her shoulder. Natasha cried. She was struggling with trusting God. I felt her pain.

Have you ever felt like that? Have you hoped and trusted in God for something only to be disappointed? Have you prayed so hard for God to move on your behalf only to feel rejected? Are you going through this stage right now? You're not alone, sis! We've all gone through this stage. The stage of silence. The stage where we feel like God is paying attention to someone else.

Before you conclude that God isn't listening, I need you to hear me out. We often pray and desire things we think we need. We live like we know what's best for us since we know ourselves. But do we? We want God to always say yes to every question. We TELL God what we want. The problem with this is that we do not ASK God if our desires are in alignment with His. Alignment? Mercy, what are you talking about? Sis, we need to constantly be in alignment with God. We must make sure that we are positioned correctly. We have to be in line with where God wants us to be. It is only when we are in alignment with God that our requests align with His desires for us. It is only when we seek Him in all areas of our lives that our requests sync with His. When we spend time in His presence, He reveals our needs, and He provides them for us. He brings our attention to what we ought to want. He exposes the reasons behind our lack of certain things. When we are in alignment, we find peace and trust in Him. We have to be okay with not being "All-knowing." That title does not belong to us. We have to find peace in the unknown.

Peace only comes when we allow God to work as He deems fit. It's not easy, but it's possible. True peace comes when we surrender. Our surrender is our trust. We surrender because we want to trust Him. We surrender for many different reasons. We surrender because we have no choice. We surrender because we lose hope. We surrender because it's our only option, and we surrender because we choose to believe. Whatever your reason is for surrendering, surrendering leads to peace. We have to embrace that peace.

Consider when you were a child. You were not knowledgeable enough to control your life. You had no clue of what would happen the following day. You just relaxed and took every day as it came. There were times when you fell, times when you got hurt, but that didn't stop you from getting up again. That didn't stop you from continuing the adventure. As a child, you had dangerous faith. The faith that didn't know the definition of fear. The faith that could walk on water. The type of faith that your parents couldn't understand at times. This is the faith and trust you need right now. The faith and trust that allows you to take off the seat belt, move over to the passenger's seat, and allows God to take the wheel. The type of faith that pushes the seat back and puts the window down, allowing the breeze to hit your face while you relax in the passenger's seat. Be the passenger that is not concerned about the driver's ability to get you to your destination safely. Forget about looking at the map or the GPS. Forget about taking over the wheel. Just rest, relax, and trust the process.

Where am I going with this? Beloved, we must understand that God answers every prayer request that we have. There are no requests of the saints that go unanswered. God answers. His answers are "yes," "no," or "wait." We all want to hear "yes." We get excited when God answers our prayers. We scream, shout, and rejoice when God does what we want. But this isn't always the case. There are times when the answer is "no." We may never know the reason He sometimes says, "no," but we can be certain that we didn't receive it because it wasn't meant for us. We didn't get it because God had something better in mind. We didn't get it because God chose not to give it to us (yet), and we have to be okay with that. We have to get rid of the mentality that we deserve certain things for certain reasons. God owes us nothing!

Whatever we get is because of His grace towards us, His abundant grace.

Then there is "wait." The "wait" answer is often silent. The waiting season can be frustrating because we don't know what's going on, and there's nothing we can do about it. We don't know if God will say yes or no. We don't know how long it will take. The only thing that we can do is to succumb to the process and wait.

Let's go back to Natasha's case. Natasha felt that God disappointed her because He did not answer her prayers concerning her best friend, Jennifer. She had trusted that God would answer her. She believed God would keep her friend alive. But God did answer her prayers! His answer was "yes!" His "yes" just had a different definition and interpretation from Natasha's. God said yes! Yes, I will give her life, life in eternity. Yes, I will take away her pain so that she will suffer no more. Yes, I will keep her forever. I explained to Natasha that although Jennifer was no longer with us, that did not mean that God stopped answering prayers. I told Natasha that Jennifer's physical death was a spiritual birth into eternity.

Now I know there are no perfect words to comfort someone after a loss. I know there is nothing I can say to fill the void, but I do know the God I trust is able to fill every void. I know that He has the perfect words, and because of this, I can confidently point those who are grieving back to the

Father. I want to do the same for you. I want to point you back to the Father. I don't know what you have lost. I don't know what struggles you're going through now, but I do know that you can trust God to make ALL things work out for your good. He has a track record of being the only One who has never and will never fail. You can trust that whatever answer He gives you is perfect, even if you don't see it now. So, if you've been searching for a new job and you haven't got it yet, keep trusting. If you feel you should be married by now, but it hasn't happened for you yet, keep trusting. If it looks like God isn't there, keep trusting. Keep trusting, sis. He hasn't forgotten about you.

Now, I also told you that Natasha was grieving the disappointing response she received concerning her application. You see, this was Natasha's third rejection letter. She told herself that if she didn't get in this time, she wouldn't try again. She connected the rejection letter with God's rejection. I had to stop her in her tracks. If you've been doing the same thing, I'm here to stop you in your tracks as well. Human rejection is not God's rejection. Just because the world says it's over for you does not mean that it's over. Stop believing those lies over your life. Don't allow a few "nos" to stop you from living your best life. See every disappointment is a lesson, an experience. A chance to do better. A chance to try harder. The grace to prove to yourself that you are stronger than you thought. This is not fiction; it is a fact!!! You are stronger than you think, sis! If you are still alive, it is because God has more to pour into you. God has testimonies with your name on it. God still has blessings stored up for you. If God hasn't given up on you, why give up on yourself?

Imagine a broken vase that the potter decides to fix. He takes his time and molds it back to normal. He brings it back together and recreates the treasure that it once was. The only change in this vase is that it has sealed cracks, but funny enough these cracks bring out a previously unseen beauty. This vase has a story! This vase is not just an ordinary vase. This vase has experienced pain. It has been damaged. But it is still useful for greatness. It is still a treasured vessel. The fact that the potter took his time to put the vase back together clearly shows that he still wants and needs the vase. The potter cherishes the vase. The potter refuses to give up on his handiwork.

Sis, you and I are the vase, and God is the potter. He is not done with you yet. He still has plans for you. You are a valued treasure. You may be broken, but He can put you back together. He can make you whole. There is no other answer but Him. If you run to drugs, sex, the streets, or whatever else, they will only give you temporary satisfaction. A broken vessel is still useful for mighty works. The Lord has a need for you, sis! Don't give up because you haven't reached your desired goal. Greatness takes time. If you haven't gotten there yet, it is only because God is still preparing the place of satisfaction for you. God is still on your case. Slow progress is still progress. Don't let anyone fool you. Just because you haven't reached the finished line doesn't mean you should forfeit the race. Keep pushing, sis! I need you to keep trying! The world needs you to keep going! Your decisions will impact someone's life. Don't stop, sis.

There have been so many times when I wanted to quit. I remember when I was in nursing school, I had this teacher who was said to be the worst teacher in nursing school. No one wanted to be enrolled in her class, but none of us had a choice. Every student had to pass through Dr. Jamison's class (I changed her name to protect her identity). I remember a specific day when we all had to take the Health Education Systems, Inc (HESI) exit exam. During that time, I was going through so much personally, but I still strived to study for the test. I was scared. Everyone was scared. No one wanted to fail. No one wanted to repeat Dr. J's class. No one wanted to spend an extra semester in nursing school.

The morning of the exam, I received some bad news, but I had a test to take, so I had to keep moving. I sucked it up and went in. When I finished the test, I did not feel confident at all. I could not remember a single question. My mind went completely blank. I went back to my room and cried. I felt helpless. Everything seemed like it was falling apart. I couldn't hear from God. I didn't feel His presence. He was silent; at least that's what I thought. The following day I found out that I had failed the exam. I didn't think my life could get any worse. I was ready to graduate, and now I couldn't. Most of my friends passed the exam, but I didn't. "*Where are you, God?*" I thought. *"I studied, I prayed, I cried, and still yet, you didn't let me pass God. Why?"* I couldn't stop crying. My life was falling apart before my eyes, and there was nothing I could do.

Everyone believed that Mercy was the strong one, so I tried to hold it together and not let anyone see my tears. I was the one that held people together when they were falling apart, and now that I was going through my little ordeal, there was no one for me to cry to. I had to be strong! One night, I prayed. I asked God to speak to me. I asked Him to forgive me for doubting Him. I asked Him to help me. That night, about three weeks later, I clearly heard the words, "Trust me." There was peace in the voice that I heard. The peace fell on me, and I felt a calmness, a peace, a feeling of ease. I knew it could only be God. I laid down and slept. The following morning, I woke up, and I felt different. I can't tell you exactly how, but all I know is I felt different, a good kind of different. Did I still have to repeat the class? Yes. Did I graduate that semester? No. But I still felt at peace. I had moments when I felt like giving up. I had my moments when quitting seemed like the easiest decision that I could make, but I chose to fight. When I felt like quitting, the people in my circle pushed me! When no one was around, I cried and prayed; but I refused to lose. I refused to give in. I had come so far, and I wasn't going to let the enemy have the final say.

I can look back and tell you the testimony because my tears were my prayers, and they prophesied victory for me. They were tears of pain on those hard nights, but my tears became my unspoken prayers to the Lord. He heard my cry, and I graduated the following semester. I went from someone who wasn't supposed to have one degree to a confident woman with three degrees and one in the works! My tears did not go to waste. God held my tears in His hands and turned them into testimonies that others can now draw from. I was a well of bitterness, and now I stand as a well of everlasting joy because I allowed God to fill me up. I allowed God to have His place. Others can now draw from my well because the Lord is the One who fills it up. I am complete because He completes me. The truth is, neither my husband nor my children "complete" me. My career does not complete me, no! My completion comes from the Lord, and because He completes me, I can pour into others and help them where they are struggling.

I told Natasha the same story I'm telling you. You cannot give up. No! No! No! If I have to repeat this a million times, I will. I need you to realize that you can't quit. You have fought hard enough to get to this stage. You can't stop now! Trust in the Lord with ALL of your heart (no matter the circumstance or situation) and *lean NOT on your own understanding. Acknowledge Him in all your ways and He will direct your path*[xv]. When you fall, trust that His plans for your life are greater than the plans you have in mind. When things don't work out right, trust that His path is clearer than you can imagine. When you feel alone and don't know what to do, trust in the One who created the beginning from the end. Yes! The God you serve is that great. He went to the end of your life and created the beginning. He knows it all. Run to Him, run into His arms. He is waiting for you to surrender your all to Him. Surrender every struggle, every rejection, every addiction, every fear, every doubt, and all the piled-up anger. Surrender it, sis! Surrender it now.

Sweet Jesus, I pray for my sister. As she has read these words, make it easy for her to surrender it, Lord. Help her to lay it at Your feet. Cause her to be at ease as she chooses to give it all to You. Remind her that trusting in You is the best decision she can make.

Make a choice today. Sis, you cannot be lukewarm. It's either you trust Him, or you do not. There is no in-between. I know you got it, sis, but how is all that weight on your shoulders? What about those nights that you stay up crying? I know those nights are hard. How are you coping with the stress of balancing everything? The load is heavy, right? That's because it's not meant for you to carry. It's not your fight; it is the Lords. He's got you, babe! Trust Him.

Before I move on, I want to pray for every one of you who is struggling with some sort of bitterness. The Lord is telling me that some of you are angry, upset, bitter, and just sad. There are some of you who are upset with the Lord because you didn't get what you asked for. Yes, I'm talking to you, sis. I know you did everything right, and you believe that you deserve what you are asking God for. Sis, please don't give up. God did not reject your request. I know it may feel like it, but the truth is–He has something better in store for you. His plans for you are so much better than you can ever imagine.

So, I pray for you today that God will take away your bitterness and give you joy. I pray that you receive understanding for the season that you are in. I pray that you let go and let God. For my sister who lost her mother, *I pray that God overwhelms you with His love, so much so that you are able to see that she is cheering you on from the clouds with a big smile on her face. I pray that God opens your eyes to see that she has just transitioned to a different address. She is not dead, rather she is more alive than you can ever imagine, and I pray that God reveals that to you.*

I pray for my sister who is struggling with being dumped by her boyfriend. I see you, sis. I know he has moved on, and you're still dealing with the hurt, but I stand in the gap for you, sis. I pray that God fills the void that you are experiencing. I pray that God shows you why that man wasn't for you. I pray that you are reminded of God's promises to you, which are yes and amen. I pray you remember that He has your life planned out for you, and in due season, He will bring the one He has chosen for you.

I pray for everyone suffering with the guilt of her past. I pray that you forgive yourself and release it to God today. I pray that you experience freedom, and from today, you walk as the liberated person that you are. I pray this in Jesus' name.

CHAPTER 14

Defeat The Enemy Within

Alright, sis. Let's uproot some buried restraints that refuse to let you go. There are some dark secrets within you that have been challenging your sanity. You know those secrets that no one knows. The secrets that keep you up at night. The secrets that make you feel like God can and will never forgive you–yeah, those secrets. I want to help you uproot these secrets so that after you put this book down, you can begin to own what the Lord has given you. I want you to destroy these thoughts so that they no longer keep you bound with chains in the dungeon. I know a young lady who struggled with this, and she has given me permission to share her story so that it will help set you free, just as it set her free.

Naomi and her siblings grew up in a very strict home, and everyone knew it. Because Naomi was unable to do anything without her parents' consent, she decided to become a rebel. Everything that her parents told her not to do became her desire. At the age of nineteen, she found herself pregnant by a married man. She did not know what to do or how to handle her current situation. The man who impregnated her told her she had to abort the pregnancy because he didn't want his wife to find out, and he was already happily married with children. Naomi felt alone. She could not tell her parents what she was going through, and she could not confide in anyone. Naomi decided that the right thing to do was to abort the baby without her parents knowing, and that is exactly what she did.

Naomi struggled with her relationship with God because of her past. She felt like God would never forgive her because she coveted someone else's home; she slept with someone else's husband, and she had taken the life of an innocent child. Naomi was broken and hurt. She claimed to be a Christian but had no relationship with God. She went to church and tried to be active in every way possible. However, she was still struggling at night with the thoughts of not being worthy enough. These thoughts kept her bound for several more years. She found herself in abusive, controlling, and unhealthy relationships.

I happened to be at an event and was introduced to Naomi by some ladies. I could see the pain in her eyes. She spoke for a little while, and then we exchanged numbers. Fast forward to a couple of months later. Naomi shared her dark secrets with me. We talked, prayed, and just gave it to the Lord. Over the next few weeks, we studied the scriptures, and we worked together on identifying her self-worth.

I know you're probably expecting me to say that Naomi lived happily ever after, but it's not as simple as that. Naomi had to learn to lean on God. She had to reject the enemy's thoughts. Naomi had to recite affirmations over her life. That is exactly what I want to tell you. The enemy is good at playing with our thoughts at night and even during the day, at times. He finds extreme enjoyment in playing with the things that we have not told anyone. He uses our past to try to hold us down. He uses our past to shame us, to tell us we are not enough. He uses our past to scare and threaten us. But, we will no longer allow him to do those things. Do you know those thoughts that creep up during the night? The thoughts that cause you to have sleepless nights. The thoughts that strangle you to the point where you feel like giving up. The thoughts that make you feel like you don't deserve better–yeah, those are the thoughts that we want to destroy today. They are the past, and that is where they need to stay. So how do I let go of them, Mercy?

1. Expose them.

Yes, I came right out with the most challenging part. There is no need to sugarcoat anything at this point. You're my sis, and I have to be honest with you! I know this sounds harsh, but just hear me out. The enemy is able to play on your thoughts because they are in the dark. Anything kept in the dark is available for the enemy's prey. So, it is really important that you let it out. You don't have to go around the world exposing your secrets, but I want to encourage you to find someone you can trust. The person who you choose has to be someone that can support you in prayer. Someone that can lift you up when you are down. Someone that can remind you of your worth and who God has called you to be. This person might be your sister, your mentor, your accountability partner (if you have one), your pastor, or whoever you know that can support you in the areas listed above. Find this person and tell them what you are struggling with.

2. Forgive yourself

Sis, you have to forgive yourself. I know you feel guilty. I know you feel like you betrayed yourself or someone else, but it's time to let it go. Living in purpose requires you to let go of the past. Your purpose is not your past. Your past is a step that occurred, but it does not determine who you are, and you have to know that. You have to be willing to forgive yourself. Listen, Jesus forgave you. He gave His life as a ransom for you, and you need to receive that. I don't know if you're saved, but once again, I want to give you the opportunity to give your life to Christ. When you give your life to Christ, He breaks the chains! He gives you freedom! He stops the oppressor in his tracks! But you have to accept Him in your life. Will you give your life to Christ today? If so, recite this prayer with me now:

Dear Father,

I come to You today full of sin and guilt. I confess my sins before You today. I ask that You forgive me for every sin that

I have committed. I confess with my mouth, and I believe in my heart that You are Jesus, the Son of God. I believe that You died and rose just so that I can have a chance at eternal salvation. So today, Lord, I give You my life. Take it and use me as You will. Release me from all bondage as I surrender to You today, in Jesus' mighty name. Amen.

If you said that prayer, I want to welcome you into the family of Christ! Welcome! Please email me at welcome@adamselsdiary.com so that I can celebrate with you.

Alright, sis, you have taken the biggest step. You have asked for forgiveness, and Jesus has forgiven you. Now, will you forgive yourself? Will you allow yourself to be detached from the sins that have kept you bound? The ball is in your court, sis! You have to say, "I AM FORGIVEN! I FORGIVE MYSELF." Say it! Say it out loud.

3. Denounce it.

Stop reliving the offense. You have to let go of the past. You cannot allow yourself to relive what no longer exists. So, this is what I want you to do, every time you have a negative thought, every time you remember something about your past that has previously haunted you, I want you to stop the thought in its track. Do not, and I repeat, do not allow the thought to play out in your head. There are times when we allow ourselves to internally lounge around in our past and replay it over and over again. This is not acceptable! You cannot live that way anymore. You are now a new person!

So, when that thought comes to your mind, say out loud, "That is no longer me! I have been saved by the blood of Jesus. This thought is not of the Lord's, but of Satan's and I bind it in Jesus' name." That's it! You might want to grab a post-it and write those words on it. Once you do that, put it in the place where you notice you often think a lot.

There is also a scripture that I hold dear to my heart, and I want to bless you with it as well. It is 2 Corinthians 10:4-5 AMPC:

*"For the weapons of our warfare are **not physical** [weapons of flesh and blood], but they are mighty before God for the **overthrow** and **destruction** of strongholds, [inasmuch as we] refute arguments (**imagination**) and **theories** and **reasonings** and every proud and lofty thing **that sets itself against the** [true] knowledge of God; and we lead **every thought** and **purpose** away captive into the obedience of Christ (the Messiah, the Anointed One)."*

The King James Version of 2 Corinthians 10:4-5 reads as follows:

*"(For the weapons of our warfare are **not carnal**, but mighty through God to the **pulling down** of **strong holds**;) 5. Casting down **imaginations**, and every high thing that **exalteth itself against** the knowledge of God, and bringing into **captivity every thought** to the obedience of Christ."*

Now, sis, you need to either write this scripture out or print it out. You can check out the other translations and write whichever one resonates with you. Whatever you do, make sure you have this posted by your bed. Memorize it so that you can recall it anytime you need it. Say it out loud.

4. Affirmations.

Now, sis, I'm sure you have heard about affirmations before. They are needed, and they are powerful. Especially the affirmations that are centered on the word of God. I need you to work on some affirmations and recite them every morning. When you recite these affirmations, they will help you manage the thoughts that try to come and attack you. I will give you five affirmations now, and then you can search the scriptures for more affirmations. *A Damsel's Diary* will also offer affirmations in 2021 so that you can add them to your collection.

a. I am precious to God, and He will take care of me (Isaiah 43:4NLT).

b. I have been created for such a time as this. I am chosen. I have a critical purpose to fulfill on earth (1 Peter 2:9).

c. Because the Lord is my Father, I lack nothing (Psalm 23:1 NLT).

d. My life has been designed by the greatest architect. I am authentic (Psalm 139:16 NLT).

e. I am more than a conqueror (Romans 8:31 NLT).

Now I want you to rewrite these affirmations on a post-it. Stick it on your mirror so you will see it every day. Recite these words out loud. You may not believe it, but the more you recite it, the more you will believe it, and the more you believe it, the more you become it. Be intentional. It is necessary!

These are the steps that I helped Naomi work on when she was struggling, and she now lives guilt-free. Do the negative thoughts try to arise? Yes, but she has all the tools she needs to destroy them. Listen, sis, this life is not a smooth ride, but when you have Jesus, He carries you through the bumps and turns. So, I want to encourage you to practice these steps that I have discussed today and watch the Lord help you. Sis, these tools are your weapons against the enemy, as well as the attire that you must decide to put on daily. What attire am I talking about? Ephesians 6:12-18 says:

"For we do not wrestle against flesh and blood, but against principalities, against powers, against the rulers of the darkness of this age, against spiritual hosts of wickedness in the heavenly places. 13. Therefore take up the whole armor of God, that you may be able to withstand in the evil day, and having done all, to stand. 14. Stand therefore, having girded your waist with truth, having put on the breastplate of righteousness, 15. And having shod your feet with the preparation of the gospel of peace; 16. Above all, taking the shield of faith

with which you will be able to quench all the fiery darts of the wicked one. 17. And take the helmet of salvation, and the sword of the Spirit, which is the word of God; 18. Praying always with all prayer and supplication in the Spirit…".

When you have all these tools, the enemy cannot compete with you. The enemy will back down because he will see that you know who you are and whose you are. So, sis, you need to get to work. It is a daily assignment and a challenge I present to you. I have done it. Naomi has done it, and you can do it too. You have to defeat the enemy within. Beloved, there are generations depending on your obedience. You cannot allow the enemy to win. The decisions that you make each and every day will determine whether you propel into your purpose or you remain stagnant in your "here and now."

Why am I so passionate about this? I am passionate about this because I know God has called you to do something great. I also know that the enemy does not want you to understand your worth. Why doesn't the enemy want you to know who you are? Because he is afraid of you. He is afraid of every woman (and man) who knows their purpose. Imagine if everyone was to walk in their divinely called purpose. Can you imagine how afraid Satan would be? He doesn't want any of us to know who we are in Christ because he knows that once we figure out how he operates, his plans will be exposed, and it would be over for him. So, my goal here is to get every one of my sisters to know who they are so that we can all dismantle the plans of the enemy. I want everyone who dares to be great, to work out their purpose with God as the foundation, and greatness as their determination (pushing force).

So, sis, don't you dare! I know it seems like everyone is doing better than you. Every time you try, you just keep falling short. You've been going at it for years, but you haven't produced your desired result. Everyone is reaching the stars except you. You don't have the finances to execute the vision God has given you, etc. I have a quick word for you– "DON'T YOU DARE GIVE UP!"

Go at it again, and again, and again until you get it done! You have it in you to produce what God has embedded in you. I want you to remember today that SUCCESS TAKES PRACTICE! You've got to TRIP and FALL before you RISE and stand TALL!

God believes in you, and that is why He has given you this task! Go get it, WINNER!

CHAPTER 15

The Next Level–Marriage?

Once you know your purpose, you can boldly walk in whom God has called you to be, and then, you can proceed into the relationship that God has called you to. Cathy is a perfect example of this. Cathy had been through a lot of heartaches. She had been hurt, broken, abused, and used. She started dating her boyfriend at the age of twenty. They loved each other so much. Cathy knew Kevin was the guy for her, and she made sure that everyone else knew it too. Kevin loved Cathy. He never failed in showing his affection towards her in public. They dated for ten years! Yes, they had challenges here and there, but that did not stop their love.

Cathy started to get concerned when her boyfriend had a hard time securing a job. He wasn't able to hold down a job because he wanted to be an entrepreneur and his goal was to focus on that. Cathy was ready to settle down, and Kevin had promised to marry her. So, she stood by her man and waited for him to get it together. There was no way she would leave him because she had invested ten years of her life with him. She was thirty years old now, and all she knew was Kevin. Even though Cathy had issues with Kevin's parents, she refused to give up on the relationship because she wanted it to work.

Cathy prayed day and night for the love of her life. She prayed that he would realize that he needed to get it together. You see, Kevin professed his love for Cathy with his mouth, but he did not do the necessary work needed to begin planning a future with Cathy. Cathy was tired. She wanted to be married. She wanted him to have the desire to move to the next level. She wanted him to man up and do what he needed so they could get married and start a family. Kevin spoke in favor of marriage, but his heart was not fully there.

Cathy decided the best thing for her to do was to break up with Kevin. She knew Kevin loved her enough that he would get his act together and come back to her. So, Cathy decided that she had to risk it all. She had to risk their relationship for the opportunity of a better future. So, she called him into the living room and told him that she had had enough of his immaturity. She told him that she needed him to man up or move on. The words hurt her as they fell from her lips, but she had to do it.

After she was done talking, Kevin turned to her and said, "…"

Watch out for the next Damsel's Diary for the continuation of this story. Sis, you don't want to miss it because it will help you navigate your next steps!

Damsel Behold Your Beauty

She is Me!

Sis, this is for you.

The woman is POWERFUL, ELOQUENT, SKILLFUL, CARING, AMBITIOUS, INDEPENDENT, and HARD-WORKING.

She may be STUBBORN at times, but don't get it twisted, she just knows what she wants, and she won't stop until she achieves her greatest potential.

She is a GO-GETTER. She is TRUSTWORTHY, ENERGETIC, STRONG, and DIGNIFIED.

She TRUSTS in her CREATOR, the MASTER of the UNIVERSE, and because of this, there is no FEAR of the future. She speaks WISDOM and walks with CONFIDENCE. She is BODACIOUS, BEAUTIFUL, and BLISSFUL. She is the PROVERBS 31 WOMAN.

She is the first to wake up in the morning and the last to sleep at night. While working through her day, she is SKILLFULLY PLANNING how tomorrow can be better for her husband, children, family, and friends.

She is a BLESSING to anyone privileged to have her. She is the perfect HOMEMAKER, WIFE, FRIEND, ROLE-MODEL, SISTER, MOTHER, and NURTURER. She goes beyond NURSING her family; she nurses those in need, even the people outside of her home. She aims for HAPPINESS and not just for herself, but for everyone around her. She makes MISTAKES, but it's only because she is not perfect, and her load is MIGHTY. No one can do what she does the way she does it. She is a woman. She is ME.

Epilogue

I have to say it again, in the process of patience, we have the opportunity to grow and experience all that God has in store for us. In patience, we learn to trust Him. In patience, we learn who God is and who He wants us to become. In patience, we learn about our surroundings and how we can impact and make a difference. Patience is significant in life because even the most important thing that we strive for–the Kingdom, takes patience.

References

[i] Philippians 4:13 NLT
[ii] Matthew 17:20NLT
[iii] Deuteronomy 30:19 NLT; Romans 12:2 NLT
[iv] Isaiah 45:1 NIV
[v] 2 Corinthians 10:5 NLT; Proverbs 23:7 NLT
[vi] 1 Corinthians 15:20 ESV
[vii] 1 Corinthians 7:32-35
[viii] Luke 10:38-42
[ix] Ecclesiastes 12:1; 3-5 NLT
[x] Isaiah 55:8-9 NLT
[xi] Ecclesiastes 11:5-6 NLT
[xii] 1 Corinthians 2:6-10 MSG
[xiii] Ephesians 1:11-12
[xiv] Matthew 12:43-45
[xv] Proverbs 3:5-6

www.ingramcontent.com/pod-product-compliance
Lightning Source LLC
LaVergne TN
LVHW010105110826
845155LV00028B/481
* 9 7 8 1 9 5 2 7 5 6 2 4 5 *